KINDLE MANual

Amazon Kindle Fire HD 8 & 10 User Guide to Master Your Amazon Fire HD Like a Pro in 2018

By Paul Weber

© **Copyright 2018 – Paul Weber – All rights reserved.**

In no way is it legal to reproduce, duplicate, or transmit any part of this document by either electronic means or in printed format. Recording of this publication is strictly prohibited, and any storage of this material is not allowed unless with written permission from the publisher. All rights reserved.

The information provided herein is stated to be truthful and consistent, in that any liability, regarding inattention or otherwise, by any usage or abuse of any policies, processes, or directions contained within is the solitary and complete responsibility of the recipient reader. Under no circumstances will any legal liability or blame be held against the publisher for any reparation, damages, or monetary loss due to the information herein, either directly or indirectly. Respective authors own all copyrights not held by the publisher.

Legal Notice:
This book is copyright protected. This is only for personal use. You cannot amend, distribute, sell, use, quote or paraphrase any part or the content within this book without the consent of the author or copyright owner. Legal action will be pursued if this is breached.

Disclaimer Notice:
Please note the information contained within this document is for educational and entertainment purposes only. Every attempt has been made to provide accurate, up to date and reliable, complete information. No warranties of any kind are expressed or implied. Readers acknowledge that the author is not engaging in the rendering of legal, financial, medical or professional advice.

By reading this document, the reader agrees that under no circumstances are we responsible for any losses, direct or indirect, which are incurred as a result of the use of information contained within this document, including, but not limited to, —errors, omissions, or inaccuracies.

Amazon Fire HD 8 with Alexa: Advanced Amazon Fire HD Manual to Help You Use Amazon Fire HD 8 with Alexa Like a Pro in 2017 7

Chapter 1: What is the Fire HD 8 With Alexa 8

Specifications 9
Operating system 10

Chapter 2: How to Set Up your Fire HD 8 With Alexa 11

Connecting to Wi-Fi..11
Registering..11
Completing Setup 12

Chapter 3: Navigation 15

How To Create A Calendar Event 16
Installing Google Play 18

Chapter 4: Alexa 22

Using Alexa 22
What Can You Do With Alexa?..23
Alexa's Features 25
Lists..27
Alarms 28
Smart Devices 28
Skills 29
Using Silk 30

Chapter 5: Reading On the Fire HD 32

Media..32
Audiobooks..34

Conclusion 36

Amazon Kindle Fire HD 10 Tablet Manual: Advanced Kindle Fire HD 10 User Guide to Master your Fire HD 10 Like a Pro in 2018 .... *37*

Introduction **38**

Chapter 1: Understand Your Kindle Fire HD 10 .... **39**

    Features *39*

    Design *40*

    Display and performance *40*

    How to charge *40*

    How to switch on *41*

    Registering *42*

    Shortcuts *46*

    Dealing with Advertisements *47*

    Changing your wallpaper *47*

    Bluetooth *48*

    Email configuration *49*

    Storage *50*

Chapter 2: Know About the Apps **51**

    Downloading Apps *51*

    Uninstalling Apps *51*

    Downloading Videos *51*

    Prevent pop-up messages when uninstalling apps *52*

    Uninstalling games *52*

Chapter 3: Entertainment **53**

    Downloading YouTube *53*

    Downloading YouTube Videos on the Kindle Fire HD 10 .... *55*

    Downloading Music *57*

    Taking Pictures with the Camera *59*

    Electronic Books *60*

    Downloading Free Books *61*

Removing Books from Your Kindle Fire *61*

Chapter 4: How to Use Alexa on Kindle Fire HD 10 63

Activating Alexa *63*

Do's and Don'ts for Alexa *64*

Activating the Hands-Free Mode *64*

Controlling Your Echo Spatial Perception (ESP) *65*

Using Alexa Commands for Audios *65*

Controlling the Volume *65*

Alexa Voice Commands for Audio books *67*

Selecting Titles to Listen to Using Alexa *67*

Setting Timer When You Are Listening to an Audiobook *68*

Some Helpful Commands for Alexa When Listening to Your Audiobook *68*

Using Alexa with Books That Are Not Audible *68*

Voice Commands for Alexa with Books *69*

Knowing Books That Alexa Can Read *69*

Books That Cannot Be Used With Alexa *70*

Chapter 5: Troubleshooting Issues 71

Connectivity issues *71*

Disable airplane mode *71*

Frequent Crashing *71*

Keyboard errors *72*

Conclusion 74

Amazon Fire HD 8 with Alexa: Advanced Amazon Fire HD Manual to Help You Use Amazon Fire HD 8 with Alexa Like a Pro in 2017

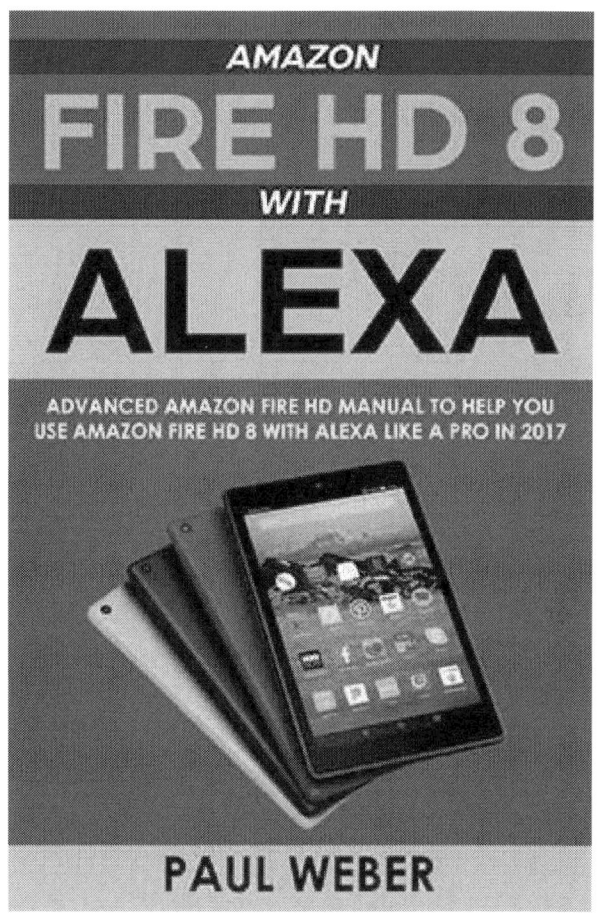

Chapter 1: What is the Fire HD 8 With Alexa

Amazon has proven that Alexa, the Amazon assistant is very helpful. However, many people wondered how well Alexa would work on the Fire HD 8 tablet because it is not always listening like the Echo or the Dot.

The Fire HD 8 is the very first tablet that includes Alexa. Instead of yelling "Alexa," as you are walking through your house, you simply hold down the home button on the Fire HD 8. This means that you do have an extra step to take when you are accessing Alexa however, this could be a good thing.

How many stories have we heard of lately of people's children saying something and Alexa ending up ordering something outrageous like a huge dollhouse or 30 pounds of cookies? So if you have wanted to use Alexa as your assistant but have been a bit afraid of having an Echo in your home due to stories such as these, the Fire HD 8 tablet may be the answer.

Alexa does make the Fire HD 8 tablet a much more capable device than other tablets so it is worth not being able to access Alexa simply by speaking.

Of course, besides pressing a button instead of speaking out "Alexa," Alexa works exactly the same as it does on the Echo devices. You will be able to use all of the same voice commands that you are used to using with Echo devices and you are going to be able to run most of the skills as well. Of course, you will still be able to run all of your smart devices from your Fire HD 8 just as you would an Echo device.

The Fire HD tablet will be used differently than the Echo devices though. It is very easy for you to ask Alexa about the weather forecast, or to turn on the lights, however, it is a bit different when you are cooking for example and your hands are covered in food. You don't want to reach over and touch your Fire HD. It is times like this that the Echo devices do come in handy.

It is understandable that Amazon would not have Alexa be voice activated on the Fire HD 8 because it is a tablet. If Alexa was voice activated, the battery would drain very quickly.

Specifications

8-inch screen (1280X800 pixels)
HD display with over 1 million pixels
1.5 GB of RAM
Quad-core 1.3 GHz processor
The choice of 16 or 32 GB of storage as well as the ability to expand the storage up to 200 GB by using a microSD.
12-hour battery
According to tests, the Fire HD 8 is 2 times as durable as the iPad.
720p HD Camera that is front and rear facing that records 1080p videos
Unlimited storage on the cloud for all of your pictures
Dolby Audio immersive speakers as well as a built-in microphone

On Deck for prime members which allows you to download the first episodes for Amazon Originals.

Operating system

The operating system is called Fire OS 5 Bellini. This operating system according to Amazon has hundreds of improvements when compared to previous versions and there are additional features as well.

The company used Android Lollipop as the base for Fire OS however, they then customized the operating system so that it is integrated with the Amazon network as well as the Amazon cloud service.

This operating system provides an improved entertainment experience giving the Amazon devices the look of a magazine. A new speed reading feature was also introduced with Fire OS 5 Bellini called Word Runner. Word Runner is supposed to help you to improve how fast you read and it does so by presenting only one word at a time in the center of your screen. According to Amazon, this helps the reader by bringing the focus to the word. The program also learns the pace that you read and it also slows down when more complex words are used.

Chapter 2: How to Set Up your Fire HD 8 With Alexa

When you receive your Kindle Fire HD 8, you are going to take it out of the box and get to using it right away, however, you will not be able to do this if you do not know how to set it up. When you turn the Fire HD 8 on for the first time, you are going to find that there are several screens that you need to go through in order to set up and register your tablet. Don't worry though, there are not a lot of questions and they are very easy for you to answer.

Connecting to Wi-Fi

The first thing that you are going to want to do is to connect to a wifi network. You will find on the first screen a list of the available networks for you to connect to. If you have an open wifi network, you will not have to have a password, however, if you do have a closed network, you will have to enter your password.

Once you connect to the internet, you will then be taken to the register screen.

Registering

Once you connect to a wifi network, you will need to register your device. In order to do this, you will simply enter the information that is associated with your Amazon account. You will need your email address that is associated with the Amazon account as well as your Amazon account password.

If you do not have an account with Amazon you will click on the "New to Amazon" link in order to create an account. This link is automatically going to take you to a screen where you can enter your name, email, and a password, creating a new Amazon account.

After you have entered your information you will then tap the "continue" button to move to the next screen.

On the next screen, you are going to be asked to agree to the terms. Make sure that you click on the link and actually read the terms. After you have read the terms, close them and you will be taken back to the registration screen. Press the 'register' button.

Completing Setup

The next screen that you are going to be taken to is the "Select Your Timezone," screen. It is important for you to make sure that you choose the correct time zone. If you do not choose the correct time zone, your time will not be correct on your tablet and this is going to cause a few different issues.

Of course, if you set any alarms or try to use your calendar to schedule appointments, the time is going to be wrong. The bigger issue, however, comes with connecting to your wifi network. If the time on the device is not the same as the time on your wifi network, you may find that you cannot connect.

If you are located outside of the United States, you are going to need to tap 'more' and then choose your time zone. Once you select your time zone, you will press the back button which is located on the bottom of the screen on the left corner. This is then going to return you to the "Select Your Time Zone" screen.

Another screen is going to appear which will ask that you confirm your account. You will press the 'continue' button. There is also going to be a link that will have your name in it. If you are not that person, for example, if you have accidentally entered the wrong information and someone else's name shows up, tap the "not (name)" and change accounts.

Once this is done, you will be taken to a screen where you can choose to connect to your social networks. All you have to do is to tap on the social media icon and sign into your account in order to connect to it.

When this is done, or if you do not want to connect to any social media sites, you will press "Get Started Now."

The next screen is going to be the first in a series which is meant to help you learn about the features that are included with the tablet as well as how to use some of the important ones. You will tap the "Next" button which is located in the middle of the screen on the right-hand side in order to navigate through the screens.

When you are finished navigating through the screens, you will press the 'close' button. This will take you to the Kindle Fire HD 8 home screen.

Chapter 3: Navigation

Working through the setup of the Fire HD 8 will help you learn a bit about navigating using the touchscreen. The navigation of the touchscreen works like most touchscreen devices. However, if you have never used a touchscreen device before, or if you just want a refresher course, here are a few tips:

1. When you are on the home screen, swipe down from the top of the screen where the status bar is located. This is going to display Quick Settings. You can then choose what setting you want to go to or swipe up to hide the settings.

2. In order to open an app, simply tap the icon.

3. Your Fire HD 8 can go to the lock screen after it has not been used for a period of time. In order to go begin using the Fire HD 8 once again, you will place your finger on the unlock button and then swipe from right to left. There is also a special offers button which you can place your finger on and swipe from left to right if you would like to check out the latest offers from Amazon.

When you are on the ad screen, if you want to go back to the home screen, simply tap the home button. The home button is in the shape of a tiny house.

4. If you need to enlarge the text on the screen, simply double tap the screen. If you want to return the text to the normal size simply tap the screen a third time. This feature is only going to work when you are using certain apps. When you are using

other apps, such as when you are reading a book, if you double tap the screen the tools will be displayed.

If you are using an app where tapping the screen does not enlarge the text, simply put two fingers on the screen and then move them apart to zoom in. In order to return the screen to the normal size, put your thumb and finger on the screen and tweak them together.

5. When you are using an app that involves going from one page to the next like the e-reader, simply swipe your finger from the right to the left in order to go to the next page. In order go back, you will place your finger on the screen and swipe it to the right.

6. When you are scrolling up or down a web page, simply swipe your finger up or down the screen depending on which direction on the page you want to go.

Using these techniques will allow you to get around the screens and navigate your Fire HD 8.

How To Create A Calendar Event

When you use the Fire HD 8's calendar app, your events are going to be synced with whatever calendar you choose to use however, you can also add events from your Fire HD 8.

Begin by tapping on the date in which you want to add the event. A new event screen will pop up. Press the plus sign. The form for the new event is then going to appear on the screen. Fill out the form with the information about the event.

You will begin by tapping on the area that says "new event." This is where you are going to type the name of the event.

Next, you will tap on the time located to the right of 'From'. You will then place the time that the event will begin in this area. On the right of 'To,' you will place the time that the vent will end.

You can skip this step and tap on the box next to 'all day' if the event is going to take all day.

Next, you will decide if you are going to place this event on your calendar in regular intervals. You can do this by tapping on 'repeat.' You can then choose weekly or monthly. This is good when it comes to specific events that you know are going to take place on a regular basis. You will simply add the event once and it will continue to appear on your calendar as needed.

Now you can choose whether or not you want to create a reminder. All you have to do to create a reminder is to tap on 'reminder'.

You can also invite those that you have saved as contacts if you want them to join you at the event.

Then you will choose 'save.' Once you save the event, it will appear on your calendar.

Installing Google Play

The Fire HD 8 is going to restrict you to only using the Amazon app store, however, because it runs on an operating system which is based on Android, you will be able to install Google Play Store and then have access to all of the android apps.

The great thing about this is that it does not even require you to do rooting which can void your warranty. After you follow the steps that I am going to give you, you will be able to access the Play Store in about half of an hour or less.

There are two different ways for you to install Google Play on your Fire HD8. The first option is a bit easier, however, because not all methods will work for everyone, I am including two. This way, if you have trouble with one option you can use the other.

Option 1-
Begin by going to your settings and then choosing security. Choose to enable apps from unknown sources. This is going to allow you to install the APK files that will allow you to access Google Play.

Next, you are going to go to the silk browser and use the following 4 links to download the APK files that you need.

http://www.apkmirror.com/apk/google-inc/google-account-manager/google-account-manager-5-1-1743759-release/google-account-manager-5-1-1743759-android-apk-download/

http://www.apkmirror.com/apk/google-inc/google-services-framework/google-services-framework-5-1-1743759-release/google-services-framework-5-1-1743759-android-apk-download/

http://www.apkmirror.com/apk/google-inc/google-play-services/google-play-services-9-8-77-release/google-play-services-9-8-77-230-135396225-android-apk-download/

http://www.apkmirror.com/apk/google-inc/google-play-store/google-play-store-7-0-25-h-all-0-release/google-play-store-7-0-25-h-0-android-apk-download/

In order to download each of the files, simply follow the link, scroll down the screen and then choose "Download APK."

When the download starts, there will be a pop-up appear. The pop-up is going to tell you that the file could be harmful to your device. Tap OK and don't worry the file will not harm your device.

Continue to do this for all 4 files.

Once you have downloaded all 4 files, close the silk browser. Next, open up your file manager. It is labeled "Docs" Go to 'local storage." Then choose 'downloads.' The four files that you downloaded will be in the download file. Tap one at a time in order to install them. Make sure that you open than in the order that they were downloaded which should be the same order that they are listed in.

Once you click one of the files, you will be taken to the next screen where you will choose install which is located at the bottom of the page. Repeat this for each of the files.

Once you are done installing all of the files, the Play Store app is going to appear on your home screen. Tap on the icon and you can then sign in using your Google account.

The Play Store may not work perfectly right after you install it, however, if you give it a bit of time (sometimes as long as 10 minutes) it will update and run normally. Now you can search for whatever app you want to use.

Option 2-

If you find that option 1 does not work for you for some reason then you can try option two which is a bit more complex but works.

In order to use this potion, you are going to need a PC as well as a USB cable. There should have been a USB cable included when you received your Fire HD 8 and it will work perfectly fine.

First, you will go to the settings on your Fire HD 8 and choose 'device options' which is located under the device option. Find the serial number and then tap on that field repeatedly. It may take more than 7 taps but soon it will show 'developer options.' Chose the 'developer options'.

Next, scroll down until you see 'enable ADB.' Tap it in order to enable it. Normally this is a feature that only developers use so you are going to have a warning pop up and you will have to agree to that warning if you want to continue with this option.

After you have enabled the ADB, use your USB cable to connect the Fire HD 8 to your PC. Windows will detect that you have connected the device and the necessary drivers will then be downloaded.

Once the drivers are downloaded, you will go to http://rootjunkysdl.com/?device=Amazon%20Fire%205th%20gen&tag=823814-20 on your PC and then download Amazon-Fire-5th-Gen-Install-Play-Store.zip". Unzip the file after it is downloaded and then open the 1-Install-Play-Store.bat in order to get started.

On your Fire HD, you will see a pop-up that says, "Allow USB debugging?" Choose 'OK.'

When this begins it will go to the first screen where you will type the number 2 and then press enter. This will allow the tool to know that you want it to install the Play Store.

The app will then be installed on your Fire HD 8. Once this is done, you are going to be asked to reboot your tablet. Do so by tapping okay. Unplug the USB cable from your PC and tablet. Go back and disable the option 'Enable ADB' as well if desired.

You will find the Play Store app on your home screen. You can then tap on the app and log in using your Google account. Just as with the previous option, the app may not run properly at first but it will update itself in about 10 minutes and run normally.

Chapter 4: Alexa

The Echo made Alexa one of the most popular virtual assistants out there. Alexa can help you with everything from scheduling appointments to checking the traffic conditions to turning your lights off in your home. It is the perfect virtual assistant for everyone out there and everyone can find a use for Alexa.

Alexa is the Amazon version of Siri and is available for use on the Fire HD 8. Alexa on the Fire HD 8 is a bit different than on the Echo devices because Alexa is not always listening. When you use one of the Echo devices, Alexa listens for you to say the trigger word. However, when you use Alexa on the tablet you do have to press the button.

As mentioned earlier, having Alexa listen all of the time could be a bit problematic therefore ensuring that you have to press a button to activate Alexa could actually work in your favor.

Another great feature that the Fire HD 9 offers that the Echo does not is the screen. Since the Fire HD 8 does offer a screen, Alexa is now able to show you any relevant information that pertains to the question that you have asked.

Using Alexa

Alexa is able to do all of the basic tasks as soon as soon as you take your Fire HD out of the box. This means that as soon as you sign in, you can begin asking for Alexa to look up facts or complete conversions.

Once you have sat up our Fire HD 8 you will be able to visit Alexa.amazon.com in order to start adding skills which we will talk a bit more about later.

The initial version of Alexa does have a few limitations. You are going to have to enable 'always on' when you first launch Alexa.

In order to activate Alexa, you will tap and then hold the home icon on your Fire HD screen. The home icon looks like a tiny house. Once Alexa 'wakes up' you will say your command. You do not have to say "Alexa" as you do when you are using one of the Echo devices.

One of the great things about having Alexa right on your tablet is that she can go wherever you go which means she is always available for you to use as long as you have access to wifi.

Of course, you should not expect Alexa to perform as she does no the Echo devices. For example, you can ask Alexa to play Christmas music, while Alexa will play Christmas music it may take about 30 seconds for it to start. On the other hand, when you use an Echo device the music starts immediately.

What Can You Do With Alexa?

Alexa is great when it comes to making sure that you have all of the timers that you need. All you have to do is tell Alexa to set a time for a specific amount of time. If you need to know how much time is left on your time, all you have to do is ask Alexa. This ensures that if for example, you have a kitchen timer set, you can go into another room and work on something else without having to worry about missing the timer and burning your food.

Alexa also allows you to order items off of Amazon without ever having to visit the website. If you notice you are running out of diapers, just tell Alexa to order more. You will see a picture of the item and then Alexa is going to ask you if this is the item that you want to buy. This does give people some peace of mind in knowing that Alexa is not going to order the wrong item.

When you use Alexa on the Echo devices you can ask about the weather but when you use Alexa on the Fire HD 8, you can see the weather forecast. When you ask Alexa about the weather, a weather card is going to appear on your screen. You can then scroll down the card and see all of the weather information for the entire week. It is much like the information that you would get if you were to run a weather app.

You can use the Automatic Voice Cast to find out what is happening on your Echo device. For example, you can check to see what music someone is listening to and so forth. While this is not an extremely helpful feature it is interesting.

Of course, the tablet with Alexa is going to play music or update you on the news whenever you ask but Alexa will also let you listen to podcasts. If the podcast is available on TuneIn, Alexa will play it on demand. If you want a different episode from the latest, you will have to do this manually though.
Alexa on your Fire HD 8 will be able to turn out the lights just as if she would on the Echo devices. We will talk more about

the smart devices such as lights that Alexa can control a bit later.

Alexa's Features

In order to activate Alexa on the Fire HD 8, you will tap and then hold down the home icon until a blue line appears on your screen. When you see the blue line you can ask your question or give your command.

When answering a question, Alexa may provide you with a visual. In order to exit the visual, simply press the back button and the visual will be removed from your screen.

You can turn Alexa on or off by swiping down from the top of your screen. Once the quick settings are open you will choose settings, then device options then Alexa. When you tap Alexa you will turn the virtual assistant on or off.

If you have the parental controls enabled on the Fire HD 8, Alexa is going to be automatically disabled. Alexa will also be disabled on any child profiles.

You can listen to media and music by telling Alexa to play it for you. For example, you can tell Alexa to 'Read (and then the title of a book)' or 'Play (and then the name of a song)'. When Alexa is reading a book the text is not going to appear on the screen.

When Alexa is playing music or reading a book, the controls are going to be on the screen so you can pause the music or book.

Alexa will also allow you to play videos as well. You can ask Alexa to find a certain movie or a television show. You can also ask Alexa to show you movies that have a certain actor that plays in them or that are a specific genre.

Of course, Alexa can provide you with the answers to your questions, the news, the weather, and the traffic conditions.

Alexa can also help you to update your calendar. You are able to link your supported calendar to Alexa via the app. Once you do this you will be able to ask Alexa about any upcoming events as well as use Alexa to add new events. You can link one calendar from each of the supported calendars, for example, Apple, Google, and Microsoft Office 365.

In order to link your calendar, you will first launch your Alexa app. You will then go to the menu and choose settings. Next, choose the calendar. Find your calendar account in the list of providers. Click on the calendar that you want to use and then choose link. You will then simply follow the instructions that are on the screen which will then allow Alexa access to that calendar.

You will have to provide your login information for the calendar that you choose to use and then allow Alexa to access the calendar.

Once you link the account you will be asked which calendar you want to use, for example, work, home, etc.

When this is done you can use Alexa to access the calendar. In order to find out when your next event is you can ask Alexa, "What is next on my calendar?" You can also ask, "What is on my calendar on Tuesday?" Or even ask about a specific time on a specific day.

If you want to add an event to the calendar you will say, "Add an event to the calendar." Alexa will then help you add the event. In order to delete an event simply say, "Delete (and name the event) from my calendar."

Lists

You will also be able to access your lists via the Alexa app. In order to make a new list, you will say, "Create a new list." Alexa will ask you what you want the name of the list to be. After you confirm the name of the list you can begin adding items to the list.

If you want to create a list using the Alexa app, you will go to the app, then select the menu and choose lists. Next, you will choose create list and manually type in the name of your list. Select the + icon and you can start adding to your list.

If you want to rename the list, simply choose the area that is located in the front of the name of the list and then choose the pencil icon. You can then type in the new name. In order to archive a list, find the list and then tap the arrow that is in front of the name of the list. Tap on archive list.

If you want to delete a list you will go to view archives and then find the list that you want to delete and tap, delete list.

You can manage your lists by saying, "Add (and then the name of the item) to (the name of the list.) Or you can ask Alexa what is on a specific list by saying, "What is on my (and then the name of the list) list?

If you ask Alexa to email you the list, she can do that as well.

Alarms

In order to set an alarm, all you have to do is say, "Set alarm for (then the time that you want the alarm to go off.) You can create a repeating alarm by telling Alexa to set a repeating alarm for (whatever day of the week and the specific time.)

After you create an alarm you can go into the Alexa app and edit it. You will from the menu choose timers & alarms. Then you will go to the alarms tab and choose the alarm that you want to edit. From here you can choose to have the alarm repeat daily, on weekdays, on weekends, on specific days of the week and you can also delete the alarm. Once you have made your changes you will tap save changes.

Smart Devices

Before you begin you will want to enable your smart home device skill. We will talk about skills next. However, before you enable the skill, make sure that you read the safety information about using smart devices with Alexa.

Next, you need to make sure that your smart device will work with Alexa. You will follow the manufacturer's directions to set up the device, connecting it to the same wifi network that

Alexa is connected to. Once this is done you will go to your Alexa app link Alexa with the device. You will download as well as install any updates for the device.

In order to connect your device to Alexa, you will go to the Alexa app. Then you will tap on skills. You can from here, either browse the devices or type in keywords related to your device in order to find the right skill. Next, you will tap enable.

If you cannot find a skill for your device, the device may not be compatible. After you enable the skill you will follow the directions on your screen in order to link the device with Alexa. Then you will tell Alexa to discover your device. Or you can go to the smart home section using your Alexa app and simply tap add device.

Skills

A skill is nothing more than the Alexa version of an app. You can use skills on the Echo devices as well as on your Fire HD 8 or any device that uses Alexa. As of right now, there are over 8,000 different skills that can be used with Alexa so you are sure to find exactly what you are looking for. If not, don't worry, there are new skills launched almost every day.

Once you add a skill to your account, you will be able to use it on all of the devices that are connected in your home. The skills make Alexa even more helpful.

Skills are not features. A feature is embedded into a tablet or other device. The skill is a third-party app which you will add to Alexa in much the same way as you would add an app to your phone. There are skills that focus on news, such as The BBC News skill, skills for social media, and thousands of others.

When you add a skill to Alexa you will find that there are many different benefits. First of all, you are going to be able to use Alexa to perform tasks using that skill. You can also use these skills to create a smart home which will allow you to view the next room via the camera that is connected, control the temperature, turn on the lights and so much more.

The skills will help make your life easier and that is exactly what Alexa is supposed to do.

Using Silk

Silk is the internet browser that is used on Amazon devices. Amazon did not use an existing browser because having their own browser allows their customers the fastest experience.

In order to use silk, you will begin at the home screen. If you are not on the home screen, tap the home icon. Next, you will tap the web icon which will take you directly to Silk. If you want to display the address bar, simply swipe down from just below the status bar.

On the bottom of the screen, you will find an options bar. The options bar includes a back and forward icon, a search icon, and an icon which will allow you to enter the site address via the onscreen keyboard.

You can display more than one page at a time by using taps. If you want to add a tab, simply tap the + icon in the top right corner of your screen. When you do this you will see thumbnails of sites that you have recently visited. Tap on the thumbnail of the site that you want to go to or tap the address bar and type in the site's address.

Silk will allow you to bookmark sites just like other browsers will. Bookmarking a site is going to allow you to find them quickly when you are looking for them.

In order to add a bookmark all you have to do is swipe down from the top of the screen just below the status bar. Then you will tap the bookmark icon which is located to the left of the address bar and looks like a ribbon.

If you want to delete the bookmark, hold your finger on the page until a menu appears. On that menu, you will choose delete. A dialog box will then appear confirming that you want to delete the bookmark and all you have to do is choose OK.

Chapter 5: Reading On the Fire HD

When you tap the books icon on your home screen you will be taken to your books library. The library is going to contain all of the content that you have downloaded under the device tab. The content that is located on the cloud will be found under the cloud tab.

The tab which you are using will appear orange. You will also see a store button which if tapped will take you to Amazon so that you can get more books.

If you tap the menu button you will be able to choose how you want your books displayed. You can choose grid or list. You can also choose how you will sort your titles by pressing the buttons located near the top of the screen. You can choose by author, by recent, or by title.

You can determine which titles have been recently downloaded because they will have a small banner in the corner of each thumbnail. The banner will read, "New."

In order to read a book, all you have to do is tap on the book that you want to read.

Media

It is likely that you are going to want to copy some of your media files to your tablet from your PC or to your PC from your tablet. This is a very simple process to do. You will connect your Fire HD 8 to your PC via the USB cable which comes with the Fire HD 8.

Then you will open the file manager on your PC and find the drive that is named 'Fire.' Open Fire. In this drive, you will see that there are many different files. Some are videos, books, pictures, music, and documents. This is where you are going to drop the media from your Pc.

Find whatever file you want to copy on your PC, right-click it and then choose copy. Go back to the Fire folder that you want to drop the media in and right click on that file. Choose paste. Of course, you can also drag the file and drop it where you want it to go.

You will do the same thing when moving files from your Fire HD 8 to your PC. When you are done make sure that you choose disconnect and then unplug the USB cable.

You can also launch subscription-based services such as Netflix, Hulu, and Amazon Instant videos. If you want to buy movies, television shows or books on the Fire HD 8 you will want to make sure that you have a wifi connection, an Amazon account, as well as a credit card associated with your Amazon account.

Once you do this it only takes a few seconds for you to choose what media you would like to purchase.

If you are an Amazon Prime member you can stream your movies and television shows to your Fire HD 8. There is unlimited streaming offered however you can also purchase movies and television shows. It is the most popular titles that you will need to purchase.

In order to watch the video, you will tap on the video icon, then the word store. Tap on the title that you want to watch and then you will choose to either rent or purchase the movie or television show.

If you plan on being offline for a while it is a good idea for you to download the video instead of stream it. That way you can watch it whenever you want.

Listening to music is also an option. You can copy music from your PC or you can purchase it from Amazon. You can go to the Amazon music library and access all of the music that you have previously purchased.

In order to play a song or an album, simply tap on the song or album. You can do other things on the Fire HD 8 while the music is playing such as reading or browsing the internet. In order to do this, you just have to tap the square 'overview' icon to switch from one app to the next.

Audiobooks

One of the features of the Fire HD 8 is the ability for you to listen to the Audible Audiobooks. You will find that there is a dedicated app just for audiobooks. If you do not have an Audible account you will be given an introductory offer.

You can purchase the audiobooks by tapping on the audiobook that you want to read and then choosing 'buy.' There are different Audible plans that will allow you to download a different number of audiobooks each month.

In order to play that audiobook, you will go to your library and the find the book that you want to listen to. Tap the play icon and start listening. It is important for you to make sure that the Fire HD 8 is connected to a wifi network or to download the book if you know that you are not going to have access to wifi for a while.

You can also change the Audible settings by opening the menu and then choosing settings. You can improve the sound of the books by choosing High-Quality Format. You can also choose to enable push notifications. It is also possible for you to change how far you want the audiobooks to jump when going forward and back. The default setting is 30 seconds. In order to change this setting, you will tap on the jump forward/back option and then determine how long you want the setting to be. You can choose anything from 10 seconds to 90 seconds.

Conclusion

The Fire HD 8 with Alexa is an amazing tablet that is going to help you do all of the things that you want to do on one simple device. The tablet is very easy to use. It can double as your personal assistant, keep your organized, provide entertainment for you and your children all day long, and it can even help turn your home into a smart home by controlling your smart devices.

Spend some time exploring your Fire HD 8 and get to know it. There are so many different features that I would never be able to cover them in this book.

This book is a simple guidebook to help you navigate your Fire HD 8. Of course, there are thousands of different skills that you can add to your Fire HD 8 which will make it that much more useful for you. There really is nothing that this amazing tablet cannot do.

I hope that this book has provided you with some helpful information and that it has helped you to learn all about your Fire HD 8.

Amazon Kindle Fire HD 10 Tablet Manual: Advanced Kindle Fire HD 10 User Guide to Master your Fire HD 10 Like a Pro in 2018

Introduction

Amazon Kindle Fire HD 10 is an amazing gadget that lives up to users' expectations. We can describe it in simple terms as faster, less expensive, and better! It has a lot of value and is termed as the best of all the Amazon Kindle Fire models. How many times have you wished you could give your Kindle Fire a command and it would start doing exactly what you told it? Your Kindle Fire HD 10 is equipped with Amazon's echo feature which supports hands-free commands.

Whether you are a technology pundit or a novice, you will be enthused by all the amazing features of the Amazon Kindle Fire HD 10. Well, that is if you know how to unlock those features.

In this how-to guide, we are going to unlock some of the remarkable features with which your Amazon Kindle Fire HD 10 is equipped.

This manual is designed to assist you in understanding the features of Kindle Fire. Read on to get all essential details.

Chapter 1: Understand Your Kindle Fire HD 10

With a 10.1" wide display screen, 32 GB storage, a multitude of features and a starting price of less than $250, the Amazon Kindle Fire HD 10 is one of the best tablets on the market.

This technological buzz gadget will not leave its users disappointed whether they are browsing the internet, listening to music, watching a movie, or doing just about anything that they enjoy doing with a tablet.

Oh, and for those ads that tend to appear on your Kindle screen that might be a bit annoying to look at sometimes, you can remove them from your home screen.

Features

Kindle Fire HD 10 a fast and responsive version with beautiful widescreen HD display. Its rear-facing camera has a 5 MP capacity for high-quality photos and 1080p for shooting videos. A 720p front-facing HD camera is ideal for making Skype calls to your family and friends. The excellent quality quad-core processor with fast speed has dual high-performance 1.5 GHz and 1.2 GHz cores for quick launch apps, videos, smooth games, and perfect overall performance. You do not need to worry about storage because you will get 128 GB of storage space. Other features include Amazon FreeTime, ASAP, Page Flip, Whispersync, On Deck, Blue Shade …and much more!

Design

It has an elegant design targeted for entertainment. It has vibrant colors with widescreen viewing at any given angle one may desire.

Display and performance

It has a beautiful widescreen 10.1" HD display. The display screen has over a million pixels. The processor is a quad-core processor with two high-performance 1.5 GHz cores while the other two cores are 1.2 GHz. They run simultaneously making its overall performance great.

How to charge

Technological gadgets normally require charging before first time usage. Therefore, a very wise rule of thumb to always apply to your new device is to charge it before attempting to use it.

There are two options available. On purchasing the Kindle Fire HD 10, it comes bundled with a micro-USB and an adaptor. Plug the micro-USB into the adaptor, and then plug it into an electrical socket to get the device fully charged. Alternatively, you can use the micro-USB to connect to your computer to charge your tablet.

I would advise you use an electrical outlet if possible to charge your Kindle Fire HD 10 because it will charge more quickly using an electrical outlet.

To charge your Kindle Fire HD 10 with an adaptor, you will need to insert the smaller end of the micro-USB cable into the slot provided for the cable on your device.
Look to the right side of your gadget to find your micro-USB cable port. It is between the headphone slot and the power button.

How do you know your device is charging?

The battery icon is at the top of the screen while an indicator light is at the bottom. When charging, the indicator light appears amber in color. When the device is fully charged, the indicator light changes to a green color.

If you do not see the lightning bolt at the top of your screen, this means that your Kindle Fire is not being charged. Try testing the charger with another device if possible, and if the other gadget works with your charger, then, you will know that there is a fault with your Kindle Fire.

If the charger does not work with the other device, then, the fault is with the charger and you will need to replace it.

How to switch on

You have gotten the charging out of the way, and you are now ready to tap your way around your feature-packed gadget.

So, let us get you all powered up!
Time to unplug your Kindle Fire from whatever charging option you had used to get it fully charged.

Press the "Power button" that is located to right side of your device. Use your finger to hold down the power button. Count to approximately four and then release your finger from off the button.

Once that is done your Kindle Fire should start booting up, and it is now time to get your device registered, along with ensuring that the correct settings are activated.

Registering

Unfortunately, you will not be able to have access to your apps and all the other wonderful features on your Kindle Fire immediately.

Why? You have to activate the different settings and register your device on Amazon platform first. Based on the speed of your internet network, this might not be a lengthy process. So, relax as I walk you through the settings activation and registration process.

A bit of great news for us is that Amazon implemented a series of steps to aid users in getting started with the activation of settings and the registration process. Your first screen will be the inviting "Welcome message" that will pop-up on your Kindle Fire screen.

You have to navigate successfully through the settings activation and registration process. At the end of the sequence of steps, your Kindle Fire will be connected to your Wi-Fi network and also registered on your Amazon account.

Step #1: Select your preferred language for your Kindle Fire using the button that is located at the top of your home screen to the left. Next, look to the bottom left of your home screen; the option is available for you to enlarge the size of the text for your device if you wish to have larger text. All you have to do is to select the tab with the words "Text Size".

After you have selected your Kindle Fire language and also the text size, tap on the option to "Continue" located at the bottom to the right of your device.

Step #2: Time to indicate your "Wi-Fi Network" of choice from the networks that are listed. It is a must that you enter your "Wi-Fi password" in the slot provided.

Once you finish entering your Wi-Fi password, select the tab "Connect." Sometimes a few seconds of waiting is required to enable the connection between your Kindle Fire and your Wi-Fi network.

When the connection is enabled, it is customary to be prompted to update the software on your Kindle Fire. Just go ahead with the update. When the updating of your Kindle Fire software is completed, your device will automatically restart. This re-booting of your Kindle Fire will take approximately five to seven minutes depending on how fast your Wi-Fi network operates.

Step #3: This stage is all about getting your device registered on your Amazon account. So that means you will need to have your Amazon account login information handy in order to get your Kindle Fire registered on your Amazon account. If you do not have an account, then you will have to sign up for one.

It will only take you a few minutes to create an Amazon account. All you need to do is to select the option on your screen that says: "New to Amazon start here."

Are you wondering why you must have an Amazon account? Well, if you want to have access to all the cool benefits that Amazon Prime and Kindle Unlimited members enjoy, then, you must have an account with Amazon to do so.

Should you decide that you are not ready to access the benefits that Amazon members enjoy and you just want to familiarize yourself with your Kindle Fire, you can opt to set-up the Amazon account some other time by tapping on the option "Complete Setup Later."

A pop-up message will appear shortly after you have selected the tab to "Complete Setup Later." The pop-up message is a reminder that you must complete setting up an Amazon account in order to access downloadable items such as books, music, videos, apps, and other items on your Kindle Fire.

If there is no swaying your thoughts because you just want to use your Kindle Fire now, then, click on the tab with the word "Skip." You will be navigated to the next step once you click on "Skip".

If you have a sudden change of heart and you decide you do want to complete the set-up process, then, select the tab "Cancel" and you will be directed to the previous step.

It is time to ensure your "Time Zone "is correct on your Kindle Fire. Most of the time, the time zone does not need adjusting because your Kindle Fire normally uses the time zone of your Wi-Fi network. Nevertheless, it cannot hurt to double check to confirm it is indeed correct. After you have ensured that the time zone is correct, look to the bottom of your device screen and tap on the option with the word "Continue."

Restoring information from a previous Amazon Kindle Fire is possible during this stage of the settings activation.
To restore information that you had on another Amazon Kindle, click on the tab that appears with the words "Restore Your Fire".

Since restoring will take more time, let's continue with the settings activation and registration. So, select the tab "Do Not Restore" to continue to the next step.

Step #4: "Family Setup" is one of the options that you will see is available for you to activate. This benefit allows you to add other adults to your account. You can also include a child's profile, up to a maximum of 4. With a child's profile, you have the opportunity to download up to 10,000 kid-friendly titles using the Amazon FreeTime Unlimited benefit. Furthermore, this benefit allows you to share books, apps, and videos that you have purchased for your child.

If the child profile is not a benefit that interests you, then, no worries; just click on the tab "Not Now." Then click on the tab "Continue" that is at the bottom of your screen to the right.

Step #5: You are now at the benefit that will allow you to enable location services. This might seem to be an appealing benefit to you; however, it can drain the battery of your Kindle Fire. Therefore, you might want to opt not have this benefit. So click on the tab "No Thanks."

Step #6: The "Backup & Auto-Save" services benefit. The "Backup & Auto-Save" gives you a level of security knowing that if anything should happen to your Kindle Fire, your files are saved in Amazon Cloud—even if your gadget gets stolen or lost.
It is customary that Amazon automatically selects all of the backup and auto-save options. Nevertheless, check and ensure all of them are indeed selected before clicking on the "Continue" button that is located at the bottom of your screen.

Step #7: Staying connected with your different social media accounts is possible when you activate "Connect Social Networks" on your Kindle Fire. Your Kindle Fire HD 10 is your multi-purpose gadget that allows you to watch your movies, read your books, etc. while still being connected to your social networks.

Scroll to the bottom of the page and click on the tab "Continue."

Step #8: Amazon has certainly rolled out the red carpet for the Kindle Fire HD 10 because even insurance coverage is being offered. This benefit will provide insurance coverage against accidental damages for your Kindle Fire under Amazon's two-year insurance protection plan. It is a nice option and it is also budget-friendly. However, for the purpose of this guide, let's take the "No thanks, continue without protection" option.

Step #9: In the settings, Amazon displays its built-in tutorial on the different features of your Kindle Fire. You can choose to browse through the tutorial by clicking "Next" each time to navigate to the proceeding slide. Or at any time during the tutorial, you might click on "Exit" to end the tutorial.

Great news! Your home screen can be seen at the end of the Amazon tutorial.

Shortcuts

We are always looking for another way to do things, especially if it will save us time and effort. So, here is another way to navigate and find what you want on your Kindle Fire. You can decide if this way suits your level of time and effort.

Tap to go to your home screen. Look to the top of your home screen, where you will see a list of tabs namely: recent, home, books, vids, games, apps, and so forth. Those tabs at the top of your Kindle Fire home screen can also be used to navigate on your device.

Take for example, the book tab will take you to books and you can easily select which one you would like to read. The vids tab will take you to your videos. "Silk Browser" tab takes you to internet browsing.

If it is the case that you are looking for a specific tab that is not being displayed directly on your home screen, just use your finger to swipe left to right or vice versa to locate the tab that you want.

Dealing with Advertisements

Some people are never happy on seeing advertisements on their Kindle Fire home screen.

How do you get rid of the advertisements that are on your Kindle Fire?

Step #1: Login to your Amazon account. Go to where you see "Hello and your name," then, scroll down to the option "Manage Your Kindle" and click on that tab.

Step #2: Look to the left for "Kindle Account" and click on "Manage Your Devices."

Step #3: You will see the icon with your Kindle Fire, Now look above the Kindle Fire icon under the caption "Special Offers" for the tab "Edit" and click on it. A pop-up message will appear explaining why the ads are on your Kindle Fire screen and also informing you that to unsubscribe you will be charged a certain amount.
Once you click on the tab with the words "Unsubscribe Now With One Click" you will be charged the fee mentioned and the ads will be removed immediately from your Kindle Fire home screen.

Changing your wallpaper

Navigate to your home screen. Then, scroll down to find the tab with the word "Settings" and click on it.

From the list of tabs that appear when you click on "Settings", select the tab "Display". Now you need to tap on "Select Home Screen Wallpaper." Your final step is to tap on "Change Your Home Screen Wallpaper." There are two options available for you to choose an image for your wallpaper. You can click on the tab with the words "Your Photo" to select a personal image that is stored on your Kindle Fire or you can select an image that was pre-installed on your device.

Bluetooth

Bluetooth pairing is available on your Kindle Fire HD 10; however, there are conditions applied to using this feature. The conditions that are applied for using the Bluetooth pairing feature on your Kindle Fire are similar to other Bluetooth pairing devices.

Rule #1: Always ensure that the device you want to pair with is compatible with your gadget, and in this case, it would be your Kindle Fire. Ensure that your Kindle Fire can be paired with wireless gadgets that have the Bluetooth feature. Some gadgets that can be paired with your Kindle Fire include speakers and keyboards.

Rule #2: Ensure that the other device that you would like to pair with is within a pairable distance to your Kindle Fire.

Enable the Bluetooth feature by swiping the top of your Kindle Fire screen starting from the top in a downward motion using your finger. Once you have swiped the screen the "Quick Settings" will be displayed. Select the "Wireless" option and then click on "Bluetooth."

You will need to click on the tab "On" to enable your Bluetooth feature. Once your Bluetooth is enabled, you will see the Bluetooth icon appear at the top to the right of your Kindle Fire screen next to the wireless icon.

After enabling the Bluetooth pairing feature on your Kindle Fire, it will start searching for other available and pairable devices. You will need to locate the tab with the words "Available Devices" and, from the list of devices displayed, tap on the gadget that you would like to be paired with your Kindle Fire. Once you click on the name of the device from the list provided, a series of pairing instructions will appear; just follow them to complete the pairing process.

Email configuration

Step #1: Go to your home screen or use the "Apps Button" at the bottom of your Kindle Fire screen. Look for the "Email Icon" among the apps on your device and then click on it.

Step #2: There will be a list of different email providers that appear under the option "Add an Account."

You need to choose the one that you have an account with, by clicking on it, and then enter your login information. You will enter your name, your email address, your password, and the description. Click on the tab with the word "Next", which is to the bottom right of your screen.

Step #3: You can synchronize your contacts at this stage, along with any scheduled events you already have on your Kindle Fire calendar. After the synchronizing is completed, you can select the tab "Save" to go to the next step.

Step #4: Click the tab with the words "View Inbox", and you will be navigated to your email inbox. If you want to read an email, just use your finger to tap on the email, and it will open.

Whenever you open an email, at the top right of your screen, three tabs will be displayed. Namely: "Delete," "Respond," and "New."

If you want to write a new email, click on "New", and if you want to delete an email, you click on the tab with the word "Delete."

Selecting the "Respond" tab will allow you to reply to the email.

Now look to the top left of the screen where you will see the tab "Main Page"; if you click on "Show Folders", you will be able to see all of your other folders such as your spam box, starred, deleted, and so forth.

If you have more than one email account that you use for receiving important messages, then you can add the other email accounts to your Kindle Fire too. To add the other email addresses, go to your inbox, and then click on the "Menu" tab that is located next to the "New" tab.

From the "Menu" tab, you will see the option to "Add Account", and you can follow the previous steps mentioned to add an email account.

Storage

To help avoid having to reach your Kindle Fire maximum storage, you can check what your available storage space is for your device.

Step 1: Go to your home screen and access the Quick Panel. Look to the right and click on "More."

Step 2: Scroll down and click on "Device."

Step 3: Click on "Storage". From there you will be able to see your available storage, along with a list of items and the amount of storage each occupies on your Kindle Fire.

Chapter 2: Know About the Apps

Downloading Apps

Step 1: Move to the "App" screen by using the "App Button".

Step 2: When you locate your app screen, you then select the "Shop" tab located to the screen's top right.

Step 3: Click on the "Search" icon and then type in the name of the app or game that you would like to download. When you find the app or game you want, simply tap on it and look for the "Download" button.

Uninstalling Apps

Step 1: Use the "App Button" or "Home Screen" button to locate your apps.

Step 2: Look for the app that you would like to uninstall. Once you have found the app, just use your finger to press down on it for a few seconds. Two options will appear. The first option is to "Add to Favorite" and the second option is to "Delete." Select the "Delete" tab, and the app is gone.

Downloading Videos

Step 1: Move to home page of your Kindle Fire HD and use the shortcut at the top to locate the "Videos" tab.

Step 2: Locate the tab "Shop" and click on it.

Step 3: Click on the "Search" icon and then type in the name of the video you would like to download. When the video you searched for appears, you can click on it and look for the download button.

Prevent pop-up messages when uninstalling apps

Step 1: Navigate to where the app is (the one you would like to uninstall).

Step 2: After you have located the app, use your finger to press down on the app, then select the "Delete" tab. A pop-up appears for you to confirm that you want to delete this app. Just click on "OK" at the bottom of your Kindle Fire screen. You will be navigated to a second screen, where a tab with the word "OK" will appear; click on that tab and your device will uninstall the app.

Uninstalling games

This is similar to the steps of deleting an app.

Step 1: Navigate to the home screen using the "Home Screen" button and select "Games" at the top of your Kindle Fire screen.

Step 2: Look for the game that you would like to uninstall from your device. Once you have found the game, just use your finger to press down on it for a few seconds. Two options will appear. The first option is to "Add to Favorite", and the second option is to "Delete." Select the "Delete" tab, and in a few seconds, the game will be deleted from your Kindle Fire screen.

Chapter 3: Entertainment

Downloading YouTube

YouTube is the hot spot to get videos of all types. Whether you want to just watch them on YouTube or download them to your device, the best part about YouTube is that the videos are completely free to use.

Step 1: Installing the YouTube app on your Kindle Fire will take a longer process. The reason is that the YouTube app will not be available in the Amazon app store because, as you can guess, this app is boring a hole in Amazon's video purchasing wallet.

With that said, you need to download an app known as "1Moble Market" – it is a free app by the way.

The "1Moble Market" app will pave the way for you to access many other apps that are not available in the Amazon App store and the Android App store.

Step 2: Go to the Quick Panel and then click on the option "Settings".

Step 3: Tap on the button "Applications.

Step 4: Click on "Apps from Unknown Sources" to enable that feature.

Step 5: A pop-message will appear. Tap on the button "OK" and then use the home screen button to return to your Kindle Home Screen.

Step 6: Tap on the button with the word "Web" on your home screen, then type in the words "1Moble Market" and click the search button.

Step 7: After the "1Moble Market" page loads, scroll down, then look to the right for the tab with the words "Scan to Download", and select that option.

Step 8: On the right there is a tab with the word "Download"; click on it. When the pop-up message appears with the tab "Download File?", you then tap on the option "OK", and the file will start downloading.

Step 9: For the app to work, you will be required to download a file manager.
Navigate to your "App Store" on your Kindle Fire. Located at the top right corner is the option "Store"; click on it.

Step 10: Type the words "File Manager Free" into the search box and click on the search icon—most of the time, it is the second option in the list. The correct software will have the words "File Manager Free"; select that tab.

Step 11: Tap on "Download."

Step 12: When the file completes downloading, click on the tab "Open."

Step 13: Now scroll down to click on the tab "Download."

Step 14: Tap on "1Moble Market" at the bottom right of your page and select "Next."

Step 15: Click on the tab "Install" at the bottom right of the page.

Step 16: You can click on the tab with the word "Done."

Use your "Home" page button at the bottom right of your screen to navigate to your Kindle Fire home screen.

Step 17: Tap on the "1Moble Market", then type "YouTube" into the search box and click the search icon.

Step 18: Now scroll down to find the official YouTube app. Click on it.

Step 19: To the left of your screen, you will see the tab "Download"; click on it.

Step 20: You can use your finger to swipe the top of your screen to watch the download process. When the download is completed, click on it.

Step 21: Located to the right of your screen is the tab with the word "Install"; click on it.

Step 22: After the installation is finished, tap on "Open", and you will be navigated to the YouTube app.

Note: You cannot login to your personal YouTube channel.

Downloading YouTube Videos on the Kindle Fire HD 10

Step 1: Navigate to your home page and click on the tab with the word "Web."

Step 2: In the search box, type in the word "tubemate.net" and then tap on the search icon.

Step 3: Click on the tab with the words "Download Handster."

Step 4: Look to your left below the tab with the word "Free" and click on the option "Download." Sometimes you have to hold down on the "Download" tab for a few seconds for the pop-up message to appear.

Step 5: After the pop-up message appears, select the first tab with the word "Open." That will initiate the download process of the file.

Step 6: After it finishes downloading, you then click on the tab "Install" located at the bottom right of your screen.

Step 7: To the bottom right of your Kindle Fire screen, click on the tab "Open."

Step 8: The pop-up message that is displaying is just explaining how you should use the "green download arrow" to get the YouTube videos on your device.

Step 9: Test your new app by going to YouTube and selecting a video.

Step 10: After the video loads, it will be located at the bottom right of the screen. There will be a huge green download arrow; tap on it.

Step 11: When the pop-up message appears, select the box with the words "Do not show me this message again."

Step 12: In the final pop-up message, you are being asked to make a choice either to download the video or continue watching.

It is my pleasure to tell you to tap on the option to download the video.
Tubemate.net comes with other benefits such as a folder tab located next to the green download arrow.

Tap to open the folder. It is in this folder that all the videos that were downloaded successfully to Kindle Fire will be stored.

From that folder, you will now have the option to change the format of your downloaded videos.
If you click on any of the videos in the folder, you will see a pop-up message appear that gives you the following options: play as video, play as music, go to YouTube, convert to MP3, save as MP3, delete file, and remove from list.

Tubemate.net is very useful when you might not have any network connection. Once a video was downloaded successfully to your device, you can watch it by going to your Apps, clicking on "Tubemate", selecting "Downloads", and tapping on any of the videos that you had downloaded.

At this point, a pop-up message will be displayed giving you two options. You can either "Start over" or "Resume playing" your video.

Note: Always return to your settings to turn off the Apps from unknown sources to avoid leaving your devices accessible to viruses.

Downloading Music

Step 1: You need to navigate to your Kindle Fire "Music" app.

Step 2: Click on the tab with the word "Store" that is located to the right at the top of your screen.

Reminder: Anything under the tab "Cloud" is what you had purchased from Amazon. Anything under the tab "Device" is what you had actually downloaded onto your Kindle Fire.

Step 3: Your Kindle Music Store products are listed based on various categories. Album deals are customarily in the first category on the page, followed by new releases. Based on your purchasing history, Amazon will also make recommendations.

Step 4: Use the search box to type either the name of the artist or the album and then tap on the search icon.

Step 5: To make a purchase, you will have to double-click on its price tab to initiate the buying process.

If you just want to make a purchase of one song from the album, then click on the name of the album to view the songs that are listed on it.

Step 6: From the displayed list, look for the song that you would like to purchase and click on price tab located to the right of the song.
When the price tab color changes to green and the word buy appears on it, tap on the green "buy" button to move to next step of purchasing the song.

For all of the songs listed, you can listen to a free 30 seconds by tapping on the "play" button that is located to the left of the song.

Step 7: A pop-up message will appear informing you that the purchase is completed, and the item is saved in your Amazon Cloud Player.

The following three options are available when you go to your Amazon Cloud Player: go to your music library to play the song, download the song to your Kindle Fire, or continue shopping.

Tap on "Go To Library."

Step 8: At this step, a pop-up message will be displayed asking you if you would like to automatically download the song, along with all future MP3 purchases that you make to your Kindle Fire.

You can select the box beside the tab with the words "Don't ask me again", and then you can click the tab with the word "Yes."

Step 9: You can find the song that you had downloaded in your music app under the tab "Device".

Taking Pictures with the Camera

Step 1: Go to your home screen and locate the tab "Photos" and click on it.

Step 2: Look to the right at the top of your screen for the "Camera Icon" and tap on it.

Step 3: You are now able to take your pictures and edit them. All you have to do is to tap on the "Camera button" that is to the left of your Kindle Fire screen, and you will be able to snap a picture.

Step 4: The pictures that you take will be at the bottom of your Kindle Fire screen. To view any of the pictures, click on it. Swipe to go to the next picture when you are finished looking at the one you had selected.

To email a picture, just look to the right side of the screen for the tab with the word "Email" and click on it.

If you want to remove a picture from your queue, use the "Delete" tab located on the right side of your camera app screen.

If you look above the delete tab to the right, you will find the folder with the option "Share" in case you would like others to know of the moments you have captured with your camera.

Step 5: Look directly below the email tab for an arrow; that is what you will use to navigate back to your picture folder.

Your picture folder contains all the precious moments that you have captured, shared, or uploaded to your Kindle Fire.

Now you can keep snapping to capture all your memorable moments using your Kindle Fire camera app.

Electronic Books

You can tap books on the Home Screen to read them. There will be a bookshelf to read the books, and you can tap right and left to turn the pages of the books. If you want to get the overview of the books in the series, you can visit the menu of each book and select different options. You can view characters, descriptions, awards, and some extras. With the help of Kindle Fire, you can quickly adjust the appearance of the book to make it easy to read. There will be a menu icon on the "Options" bar along with the cover, and you can view the "Table of Contents" and specific locations.

You can get options to add notes by holding the button on the word. You can drag numerous words and get the contextual menu. It is easy to highlight any passage by placing your fingers to get a magnifying box. On the community pages on the Kindle, you can share your thoughts. There will be a chat icon in the options that will help you to share your books and periodicals with your friends.

It is really interesting to read children's books because there is a new feature: "Pop-up" text. The text will pop-up on the colorful images and you can double-click the region to expand the text. Swipe your fingers to the right and left to navigate between the text sections. If you want to return to normal reading, double-tap the screen (anywhere) and get the advantage of normal reading.

Graphic novels will be enjoyed in the panel view just like live characters. You can magnify any area by double-tapping it.

Downloading Free Books

Step 1: Always make your way to your book app when you want books. You will be using the shopping cart at the top left; click on it.

Step 2: Type the words "Free Books" in the search box, then click on the search icon and all the free books on Amazon will be listed.

Step 3: After finding a book title you like, click on the book to select it.

Step 4: You will need to use the download option for the book to be loaded on your Kindle Fire. However, if by any chance the download option is not available, then click on the tab with the word "Buy", and the book will then be loaded onto your device for free.

Removing Books from Your Kindle Fire

It is not necessary to keep books on your Kindle Fire that you will never read again. Remember that you want to conserve your storage space. Therefore, if there are any items that you do not feel are necessary to be on your device, you should try and delete them.

Step 1: Go to your home screen to find the "Books" app and click on it.

Step 2: Check to ensure that the button with the word "Device" is on orange. If that tab is not on orange and you delete a book, you would have deleted the book from your Amazon cloud and not actually from your Kindle Fire.

Step 3: After ensuring that you are actually looking at books on your device, you can then search for the book you would like to delete by scrolling through the list of books.

Step 4: When you find the book, you will need to press down on it until you see the options "Add to Favorite" and "Delete."

Step 5: Tap on "Delete" and, in a second, the book will be removed from your device.

Chapter 4: How to Use Alexa on Kindle Fire HD 10

Give your fingers a well-deserved break from tapping around on your Kindle Fire HD 10.
Alexa is like your hands-free, command-driven, technologically handy assistant.

While the Amazon echo product was available for purchase on the shopping giant's website, it was never a built-in feature of any of its generation Kindle Fires until now. Also, when you compare the cost of the echo product by itself and a Kindle without the feature, you know you are getting a great bargain with Kindle Fire HD 10.

Once you enable the Alexa software on your Kindle Fire 10, you can ask questions that pop into your mind, and with the voice activation, your commands can just keep going. Navigating on your Kindle Fire 10 does not get any easier than with the help of Alexa.

For each question you ask, Alexa will provide you with the correct answer, which will just leave you more inspired to continue using the feature.

Even the activation process for Alexa is amazing.

Activating Alexa

Step 1: Boot-up your Kindle Fire. Use your finger to press on your Kindle Fire "Home Icon" until you see a blue line appear.

As soon as the blue line appears on your Kindle Fire, it means that Alexa is enabled and is ready to take your commands.

Yes, you can test your Alexa feature and give it a command right now.

Do's and Don'ts for Alexa

The Alexa visual display might appear on your screen. If you want to remove it from your screen, then tap on the "back" button that is located at the bottom of your Kindle Fire screen.

Naturally, if the Alexa feature can be turned on, then it must also have an off button too.
Turning off the Alexa feature on your Kindle Fire is just as easy as turning it on.

Step 1: Use your finger to swipe the top of your device screen in a downward motion. Click on the tab "Settings."

Step 2: Tap on the "Alexa icon" and it will be turned off.

Alexa is not enabled by default on children's edition Kindles or if there is a device that has a parental control feature.

If your Kindle Fire has a kid or secondary adult profile, Alexa will not work on that device.

Alexa hands-free mode cannot work with Kindles that do not have the 5.5.0.0 or later software.

Activating the Hands-Free Mode

Step 1: Go to your home screen and access the Quick Panel which is at the top of your screen by using your finger to swipe in a downward motion.

Step 2: Click on "Settings" and then tap on the "Alexa" icon.

Step 3: Click the tab with the words "Hands-Free Mode".

Controlling Your Echo Spatial Perception (ESP)

You will need to learn how to control your Kindle Fire Echo Spatial Perception (ESP) behavior because if you do not know how, it might start responding each time it comes into contact with another device that has the Echo feature.

Step 1: Use the Quick Panel at the top of your screen to locate "Setting."

Step 2: Now select the "Alexa icon."

Step 3: Tap on the button with the words "Tablet ESP Behavior."

Using Alexa Commands for Audios

Let the sound of music tranquilize your inner vessel, mediate using your motivational audios, or just listen to what your favorite author has penned with the following voice commands for your Alexa:

- Play
- Play some music
- Play the (you need to say the name of the song)
- Play some (say clearly the genre you would like to hear)
- Resume
- Pause

Controlling the Volume

Whether you need your volume to go up or down, with the following voice commands for Alexa it can be done:

- Volume up
- Volume down
- Set volume to level (clearly state the number or the level you want the volume).

Even if you need to know the title or the name of an audio, Alexa can assist with the following voice commands:

- What is this?
- Who is this?
- What song is this?
- Who is this artist?
- When did this song/album come out?

For any audio that you would like to hear again, use the following voice command for Alexa:

- Repeat this song

There are numerous voice commands for Alexa that can be used with audios, and below are a few of them:

- Loop
- Skip
- Show me my playlist
- Play me some songs I have not listened to in a while
- Play brand new music
- Play this song (tell Alexa a line in the song)
- Thumbs up (use this command for Pandora, Amazon music, and iHeartRadio when you hear a song you like).
- Thumbs down (use this command for Pandora, Amazon music, and iHeartRadio when you hear a song you dislike).
- Play songs from (tell Alexa the precise city).

- Show me (tell Alexa the exact genre) list (use this command when using Echo gadgets with a screen).
- Shuffle
- Stop Shuffle
- Next
- Previous

Need some silence for a while or just need the audio to stop, then use the following voice commands for Alexa?

- Stop
- Pause

Alexa Voice Commands for Audio books

When you are using the Alexa feature for your audio books, the control panel will still appear at the bottom of your device screen. Choosing to dismiss the control panel will not stop the audio book from playing.

To locate the control panel after you have dismissed it, you have to use the Quick Panel at the top of your screen to find it.

Selecting Titles to Listen to Using Alexa

- Read (you need to clearly state the title of the book).
- Play (you need to clearly state the title of the book).
- Play the audiobook (you need to clearly state the title of the book).
- Play (you need to clearly state the title of the book) from Audible.

Setting Timer When You Are Listening to an Audiobook

- Set a sleep timer for (you will have to tell Alexa the exact time either in minutes or hours).

- Stop reading the book in (you will have to tell Alexa the exact time either in minutes or hours).

- Cancel sleep timer

If you have a problem remembering the chapter you last read, then use the following voice command with Alexa:

- Restart

If you mess up and tell Alexa the wrong chapter, then all you have to do is use the following command to go the chapter you really think is the correct one:

- Go to chapter (tell Alexa the chapter number).

Some Helpful Commands for Alexa When Listening to Your Audiobook

- Go back
- Go forward
- Next chapter
- Previous chapter
- Resume my book
- Pause

Using Alexa with Books That Are Not Audible

You can find books that are not audible that can be used with your Alexa feature.

Step 1: Use the Quick Panel to find the "Alexa App" and click on it.

Step 2: Select the tab with the word "Menu."

Step 3: Click on the tab with the words "Music, Videos & Book."

Step 4: Finally, you can click on the tab "Books" and then select the tab with the word

"Kindle." From the drop-down menu that will appear, you will be required to select the type of device you are using, and then you will be allowed to use your Alexa feature.

Voice Commands for Alexa with Books

- Play the Kindle book (tell Alexa the exact name of the title)
- Pause
- Stop
- Resume

Knowing Books That Alexa Can Read

- You can use Alexa feature for the books you:

- Buy from Kindle Store.

- Borrow from the Kindle Owners' Lending Library.

- Borrow from Kindle Unlimited.

- Share in Family Library.

Books That Cannot Be Used With Alexa

- Comics
- Immersion reading
- Graphical novels
- Speed control narrations

Chapter 5: Troubleshooting Issues

Connectivity issues

Wi-Fi connectivity problems can be the result of many different factors. However, when it comes to the Kindle Fire, it has been discovered that the Airplane Mode is the main cause of this problem.

Recently some changes were made to the Kindle Fire settings by Amazon. The changes to settings of Kindle Fires were made in regards to turning off both the Wi-Fi and 3G connection. Kindle Fire users will have to use the Airplane Mode to disconnect either their Wi-Fi or 3G network on their devices.

Once an icon appears on your Kindle Fire screen that resembles a plane, then your gadget is in the Airplane Mode.

Disable airplane mode

Step 1: Use the Quick Panel on your device to locate the "Menu" tab.

Step 2: Click on the tab with the word "Settings".

Step 3: Tap on "Airplane Mode". Located to the right of the "Airplane Mode" button is the "on/off" button; click on it to disable the airplane mode.

Frequent Crashing

One of the main reasons for this problem is activation of the parental control features on your device which tends to block default access.

Step 1: Use your Quick Panel to locate the tab with the word "Settings."

Step 2: Select the tab "Parental Controls" and disable the parental control feature.

Sometimes clearing the history of your Silk Browser can also resolve the problem.

Step 1: Use your Quick Panel to locate the tab with the word "Settings."

Step 2: Click on the tab with the word "Applications."

Step 3: Tap on "Manage All Applications".
Step 4: Click on "Silk Browser".

Step 5: Select "Clear Data".

Keyboard errors

Suggestion 1: Your Kindle Fire screen might need cleaning, so use a microfiber piece of cloth to clean your Kindle Fire screen.

Suggestion 2: It is always good to want to protect your Kindle Fire from damages that might occur from a fall. So, you might have to purchase a case for your gadget. Look to see if the case is fitted properly on your Kindle Fire because if it is not fitted correctly, it could be the cause of the erratic typing.

Suggestion 3: You can force power-down your Kindle Fire by pressing down on the power button for about 30 seconds. After you have turned off your Kindle Fire, wait for a few minutes before powering it up again.

Suggestion 4: I have saved this suggestion for last because it is very risky for a novice when it comes to technology.

However, if you have no choice, then you will have to attempt to do a factory reset of your Kindle Fire.

Please ensure that all your files are saved in a backup system before attempting the factory reset because failure to do a backup of your files will result in your losing all your contents.

Step 1: Use the Quick Panel to access your "Setting" tab.

Step 2: Click on the tab "Device".

Step 3: Select the tab with the words "Reset to Factory Default".

Step 4: Tap on the option "Reset".

If the issue is greater than can be corrected by a factory reset of your Kindle Fire, you will definitely have to contact Amazon for further assistance.

Conclusion

These are the basic details about the Kindle Fire HD 10. This manual is aimed at making your life easier by solving problems that you might be having with different gadgets. It is time to explore more into your gadget.

Paul Weber

Check Out My Another Books

Amazon Echo Spot: Advanced Amazon Echo Spot User Guide to Help You Use Echo Spot like a Pro and Enrich Your Smart Life

Fire Stick: Amazon Fire TV Stick Guide to Help You Install Kodi on Your Fire Stick & Immerse You into The World of Your Media

Amazon Echo Show: Advanced Amazon Echo Show Guide to Help You Use Echo Show Like a Pro & Enrich Your Smart Home

Amazon Echo Dot: Advanced Amazon Echo User Guide to Help You Use Amazon Echo Dot in 2017 & Enrich Your Smart Home

Printed in Great Britain
by Amazon